# MY WORDS

## GEORGE WYLLIE'S
### ESSAYS FOR
### *ArtWork*

# My
# WORDS

## George Wyllie's

Original
*ArtWork* essays
reprinted in
one slim
volume

An *ArtWork* special
from Famedram

*Printed and published in Scotland by*
*Famedram Publishers Ltd, Ellon, AB41 9EA*
*© 1998 Famedram Publishers and George Wyllie*

To the memory of
RUTH HALL
*Writer, musician and mentor*
*who loathed the visual arts*

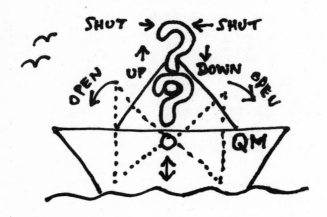

# Preface

BILL Williams asked me ages ago If I'd like to write a short article each month for his punchy newspaper, but it took some time for me to decelerate from sculptural matters to an unpredictable relationship with the mighty lap-top. This versatile gadget insisted that I impose on myself the monthly discipline of writing short essays on anything and everything, and for over a year now these have been regularly imposed on the readers of *ArtWork* and now, slightly re-worked, re-imposed by this book.

I enjoy essays, their brief content suits me very well for compact injections of wit and profundity – not least from the works of the daddy of them all, the excellent Michel de Montaigne. His example of disobedience to chronological sequence and ordered subject matter, suggests that it's alright for my keyboard to feed any subject at any time into my printer. I don't know how it did it, but it has somehow printed out... MY WORDS.

GEORGE WYLLIE 1997

# Foreword

GEORGE Wyllie has become an institution in Scotland. If it wasn't such a hackneyed term you'd be tempted to say he was an icon. *(Memo to George: a piece on icons?)*

Yet for many years for me there was something of a question mark over the man. It was, I suppose, put here by him with his scul?tural innovations. Very clever, but.

That was when I didn't know him. I really got to know George Wyllie when I sought his help in STORM'S campaign to save the Fort William sleeper. His response was typical: immediate and enthusiastic agreement; passionate support for the cause; a witty and hard-hitting image – which was reproduced around the world. And the whole venture realised from conception to actuality in a week, on a budget of little more than thin air.

But Wyllie has a winning way with words as well as images. They work for him just as powerfully as does his inspired line.

In these essays the two can be seen acting together in perfect harmony.

BILL WILLIAMS

# Voyaging beyond the bath-tub...

I
T WAS Roland Barthes who explained that the real voyage of discovery was not in the enclosed capsule of Jules Verne's 'Nautilus' submarine, but rather aboard Arthur Rimbaud's 'Drunken Boat', sailing downstream as it pleased. And so, an adventurous voyage is most unlikely in the confined waters of a bathtub, but the illusion of that possibility persists, and is comparable to art that never ventures beyond the gallery.

The intrepid voyager Richard Demarco recently made a landfall after a voyage beyond the bathtub. He had set sail over 20 years ago, setting his happy compass to follow the Celtic Spiral and, by circumnavigating the long way round by way of Meikle Seggie, he left behind the plastic ducks and the synthetic foam of convention. 'But', muttered the voices within the

bath… 'it can't be art'.

As a consequence of seeming too much like a package holiday, Demarco's pilgrim ship was torpedoed by a Scottish Arts Council who, until his decision to go afloat, had always ensured that his vessel was well found. He never quite got over being sunk by his own side, but that's what can happen if you venture beyond the tub.

All that time ago, Demarco had intuitively realised that the real adventure of art lay beyond the gallery, and the new direction had to be a journey in the company of other like minds. His gallery became the depot for fitting out and enticing a crew, and the walls were given over to reporting these explorations. His travel agent became more important than his wine supplier.

At worst, which was still pretty good, he embarked on a sea-going form of café society.

At best it was a spiralling expedition – the 'Artist as Explorer' experiencing first-hand the nature of other art and other artists in other parts beyond the seas. The creative dynamic of art was guaranteed to all who sailed with him. This art on the move was brilliant – 'performance on the move' for anyone seeking a definition. It scintillated, it was too good to be true, and too good to be funded.

He followed a route which linked the latent energy of ancient stones. First, to the invigoration of the standing stones of Callanish on the Isle of Lewis, and from there, a rambling investigative journey through Europe to the Mediterranean and megalithic temple of Hagar Qim on the island of Malta. Everywhere the energy of interaction was in the air.

The entire idea was precipitated by his unembarrassed passion to embark on an adventure of the human spirit, and to share it with others. It is now evident that no one but Demarco could have stimulated this unique art work and the journey and the creative energy it generated. It gives the clearest indication that Demarco, he of the maligned gallery, is truly a great artist.

It is nigh impossible to explain this sort of activity on an application form for funding, and yet this fundamental dynamism is essential for any art having the capacity to extend concepts beyond conventional definitions. If more definitions are required, try 'concepts on the move' or 'time-based art beyond the immediate' … but, go on, be brave, just call it 'art'.

The salty flavour of this undefinable activity was not to the taste of established art palates, and Captain Demarco had to take a lot of stick for his vision. He was compelled to play some silly games to satisfy silly rules in his attempt to survive, and he became the easy target for ridicule and rejection. Seagoing sure is tough beyond the bath-tub.

Is it the cosy comfort of the bath-tub that makes those within it disinclined to raise their vision above its rim? It's getting pretty crowded in that tub, and its easy comfort entices other bath-bound navigators to jump in. The art world could soon be sliding about in a mega-tub, blowing bubbles amongst the ducks and scrubbing each others' backs. By sheer numbers they will be able to convince themselves that this is indeed the real world, but only because of the soap in their eyes.

'An Lanntair' – the lantern, shines bright in the air of Lewis. Two decades after setting out, Demarco made his landfall near the Atlantic stones of Callanish and from thence to Stornoway where soap-suds don't stand a chance. Here the crew, smarting with invigoration, displayed their responses to the voyage and the stones, with Demarco meticulously unplanning the future.

It would have been great to have had a ticker tape parade with application forms showering down on him, and all begging the master to accept some funding... but that can only be conceptual.

# Now you see it...

I T'S surprising what happens when you confess to not knowing something that you thought the whole world knew – except yourself. If, in seeking elucidation, you have the courage to admit to this ignorance it becomes a golden opportunity for others, who also don't know, to attempt to score points by waffling that they knew all the time. An over-emphasis on unconvincing pseudo-definitions is the usual give away that indicates that they are in the same leaky boat, and so the enquirer has to seek more watertight sources.

If pressed for a genuine answer by a genuine enquirer who genuinely seeks genuine knowledge, the more honest amongst us will wearily admit to having kept their uncertainty strictly private, and had long thought they'd been solitary in their ignorance. The discovery of other such uninformed companions relieves the pent-up tension, and to have it confirmed that there is more ignorance abroad than you thought, is a great comfort. And that's how it was with me and 'Conceptual Art'.

I am happy to share with you the results of my extended random poll, conducted amongst fairly knowledgeable arty folk, as to what they thought was meant by 'Conceptual Art'? Bearing in mind that they could be telling lies, the quick definition was that it was... (i) 'ideas-based art'. Others went deeper and said it was... (ii) 'art where the idea is of more importance than the object'... and the cynics cynically said it could be... (iii) 'objects struggling to be more important than the idea'. This analysis seems to suggest that the art would be better art if it wasn't made.

An overlooked definition is there for all of us to see in *Chambers English Dictionary*... 'Conceptual Art'... 'concentrating not so much on a completed image as on the means of producing an image or concept'. This would seem to allow the validity of all ideas from Leonardo's sketch-books to wild intentions biro-ed on the back of wet beer mats. This is great news for

It's conceptual

those of us who are fed up making things anyway.

Pardon me if I'm wrong, but whether you make things or don't make things, am I wrong in thinking that all art seems to start with an idea – even if you don't know where it came from and even if the idea is not to have an idea? The free-for-all of 'ideas based art' seems OK to me, as long as one idea is not declared to be the only one that matters, and becomes bossy by insisting that this is how all ideas should happen. This can make non-followers feel rotten about having the affrontery to actually pursue very different ideas. Zooming in on a single focus surely precludes the development of all manner of ideas to allow the possibility for everything and anything to happen including nothing. Nothing of course is not quite nothing, for a conceptual nothing can be used to construct a conceptual CV.

The philosophical American avant-gardist Joseph Kossuth says something like this… "It is abundantly clear by now that we do not need to have an object to have an art work"!

If Joseph is right and his idea catches on,

we may as well fill a skip with hogs-hair brushes and half-squeezed tubes of oil-colour, send sculptors' buzz-boxes and chainsaws to car boot sales, and Damien Hirst will have to take a bad price for his formaldehyde. Only CV's will survive.

Cash derived from the sale of these obsolete tools of trade could pay for plumbing jacuzzis into redundant studios where the artists can flop, like old Archimedes, and think up ideas. When they get a concept, they should jump up, shout 'Eureka' – then do nothing about it. There could be big exhibitions about not much. A new 'jacuzzi movement' could herald the leisure age for the arts – howzat for a concept!

It's all a bit like the Arts Council which, come to think of it (and do no more than that) is already conceptual. I've always wondered why a big inverted 'V' replaces a normal 'A' in their logo. Note too that the line that bridges the middle of the 'A' is missing. Is this to encourage us to be conceptual?

Another line across another bridge was recently in danger of going missing. Someone once had a concept for building a big sculpture called the 'Forth Railway Bridge', then they spoilt the idea by actually building it.

The good news for the conceptualists is that the bridge is not all that well maintained, and if deterioration continues, it could collapse into being a concept once again.

There's only one snag – you can't run trains over a concept.

# ...Is it art, but

THERE must be some reason for the Glaswegian 'but' that turns up at the end of a remark like 'It's a great day, but'. Across the country in the ethnically different Edinburgh, they would say 'It's a great day, well'. This is a site-specific curiosity, like putting brown sauce on fish and chips in the east, and vinegar on them in the west.

Unrequired linguistic appendages can intrude internationally into greater comments than trivial abstractions about weather as exemplified by Marcel Duchamp's "The bride stripped bare by her bachelors, even". Here, the first part is ambiguous enough without Marcel adding on an 'even' at the end. Another example is Robert Burns's "man to man the world oe'r shall brithers be for a' that". You'd think that Robert would have stopped at 'brithers be' to make his point, but no, there's the afterthought of 'for a' that' – so what are the Glasgow and Edinburgh

I think it's an
erithismic itch, but

folk and Marcel and Rabbie, getting at?

These brief and intrusive expressions at the end of a statement seem to suggest some uncertainty as to its initial content being fully realised. The tentative 'but' or 'well' can be forgiven when appended to a trivial comment about weather – for in our climate no one can confidently forecast its pattern, but the ambiguous profundity of Duchamp's 'even' is not so easy to understand

Happily this ambiguity allows any interpretation, and 'even' might mean he is being artistically tentative – for that was the way of the man. Robert Burn's 'for a' that' demands wider consideration. Had he misgivings as to whether we would ever 'brithers be'? The global continuity of ethnic upheavals would certainly justify him putting Utopia on hold with an open-ended 'for a' that'.

Art, like Burn's idealism, is highly aspirational, but its loftiness and inconclusive ambiguity can suffer from exposure. It is also elusive, and what many artists think they are arting about right now might not be what they're really on about at all. If any of it is to be meaningful, the work will reveal itself in its own good time, so we just have to wait to discover if the idea articulates its value. This is a precarious ascent, for the air of lucidity can be thin and you can't hide on a narrow ledge. It could be easy to 'all fall down' – and serve the chancers right.

Awkward André Breton warned us about the danger of reaching a 'comfortable equilibrium', and that the dynamic state of liberty he recommended should be based on a continual *erethism* – the Greek word for irritation ... 'erethism'. If it's new to you, keep scratching the erithismic itch and its truth will be revealed.

André Breton – and no doubt the André of the bricks, would be delighted at the recent surge to re-charge the continuity of erethism by exhibitions of irritating art which lots of people don't think is art at all – or don't think is very good art even if they can bring themselves to admit that it could be art. There is always an obligatory outcry about modern art stirring things up, but this predictable irritation is much better than being bored – except that boredom

26

often seems to be the intention of some of the practitioners. Maybe that is what they're really after, and if so, congratulations for doing it so well.

My complaint about this trend is the tendency to exclude other like but different minds. It is as though the irritation of art has just been invented by a few, and that there was no itch beforehand. This conceit does not always recognise the link with earlier dynamisms, and the maturity of the new energies is retarded by ill-consideration of the old.

To deny art an all-embracing organic growth narrows its creative potential and is counter-productive to the very ideas that some believe can only be understood by them. I hope, but doubt, if this will irritate those who think that anyone entitled to occupy premier art space has to zoom in from elsewhere or pulsate with what old Ruskin called 'pathetic excitement'. Of course there are exceptions, but too few, and the malaise seems particularly bad when curators are in autocratic sympathy with a brat brigade, brand new from the supremacy of art colleges.

The same is probably true elsewhere, but I hope that others elsewhere will likewise irritate elsewhere, but also bear in mind the requir-ment to irritate the nearby.

If any of this smacks of self-interest let me assure you that it is just that – but it is also an expression of the frustration of mature artists. Maybe the wrinkly brigade are better off up in their attics rather than acting like geriatric hippies at a disco. Bear in mind that the Tate selectors recently had the sagacity to present stalwarts like Joseph Beuys, born in 1921 (like me, a very good year), and Louise Bourgeois, born in 1911 beating young Joseph by ten years. Louise says... 'Art is not about Art. Art is about life, and that sums it up', and so it does, and I'll disco dance with her any time!

If alternative sources of irritation are re-quired, there is no need to jet too far. Curators, here's a tip, get out and about amongst the na-tives, but there must be no attempt to measure their particular itchiness against irritation from elsewhere. If you want to curate a worry or two, there are many brave-hearts nearby to help you do it. Moreover, if any of that public which constitutes the 'life' mentioned by Louise Bourgeois, finds its way into a worrying exhibition and consequently feels inclined to protest at how much they are troubled by the experience, fear not, for out of the erethismic mist the native subversives will spring to your side. And when the fiendish doubters ask, "but is it art?", together they will nod and confidently proclaim … "It sure is, *but*."

*ArtWork 77 December 1995/January 1996*

# The drone of conferences

IT could be the first stage of hibernation, a final gasp of low energy before the winter slouch. Listen, and you'll hear the distant drone, for conference time is here again. In one month I notched up four, and I can still hear the masochistic echo of words. I missed two more, but I am haunted by an anxious conscience for not attending, and apprehensive foreboding simmers within me at the weary thought of more to come. This induced agitation makes me wonder why these compulsive gatherings can generate such drowsy angst.

Scottish sagacity doles out memorable mottoes like Patrick Geddes's "by living we learn" – so what do we learn from the conferences which periodically punctuate normally agreeable enthusiasms? Adam Ferguson, another Caledonian sage, suggested that we should "know the condition to which we aspire" – but dammit Adam, if we knew that, we wouldn't need to have conferences.

A conference is usually a disparate congregation of 'unsures' seeking the togetherness of being 'sure'. If this can somehow lead to a certainty of direction, then those gathered together will have distilled the nectar of Utopia.

I suggest that the certainty of being certain can only happen if an ocean liner is sinking, and all directional doubts are waived in favour of the quickest route to the lifeboats. This is known as expediency.

At conferences the ship always refuses to sink, for although it rolls and pitches it is only pretending to those on board that it might be getting somewhere. The uncertain expediency that I detect is the rush of passengers to the lifeboat deck to point in all directions to very interesting, slightly interesting, uninteresting, and very uninteresting observations, mostly uncertain. Anyone who has been on a Demarco voyage will be well primed in this.

Reluctance is integral to us in modifying our own views in favour of the 'interests' or 'uninterests' of others. It is also a pain in the neck to those who are inclined to ram home their expediences with above average energy. Nevertheless, the theatre of this can be a bonus, for it is awesome and pleasantly unboring to watch the expediences of others running amok.

The penalty to be paid for hearing out someone else's wild passion is the annoyance of hardly being able to splutter your own word in edgeways – and this frustration can even be compounded should another weary outburst manage to wedge itself between the previous wordiness and your intended contribution which, of course, was to be concise. Your faith in conferring then collapses, especially when the alien interjection turns out to be lengthy and boring. Conversely, one person's boredom can be someone else's passion, or even worse, their career. There is no escape from this except to put that person in the chair.

Conferences are now being seduced by the internet. We now seem to want to off-load our disparities and uncertainties on to the new technology. This has the capacity to take a big load off our minds by transferring it to a chip. It is like sweeping our crumbs of profundity under a high-tech carpet, making them appear invisible but knowing they are there all the time. Everyone is at it, and soon we'll be able to stand well back and let a minority of meaningful chips fight it out for us. Viruses permitting, there could be a microsoft star war and a global print-out. It could be one small digital step for mankind.

Evolution will have a hard time keeping up when the frenetic future beckons us to bore or unbore ourselves, with our disparities bouncing off satellites and transmitting more complicated complications than we had in the first place. All of this will depend on some global flash of lightning not striking our computers and wiping out the floppy disk.

If the screen goes blank, we can always return to Geddes's "by living we learn" – but with the following respectful amendment. If we delete 'we' and insert 'I' we will negate the possibility of yet another conference being organised for us.

The "conditions to which we aspire" might now be considered sitting on a rock far from the drone of conferences... How about Rannoch Moor, Adam?

# A sideways look at gravity

I F ISAAC Newton is indebted to the apple tree, then I am to the rabbit. This relationship was revealed when I was asked to erect a sculpture at Invernochty near Doune in Strathdon, to help the public notice the unnoticed. The unnoticed site that had to be noticed was an 800 year old Norman motte and bailey – a fortified mound.

It was truly an uphill project because Scottish Heritage insisted that no holes be dug downhill into their heritable ground to support the structure. Faced with this crisis I observed that the rabbits had unconcernedly overcome this restriction, for their holes were being burrowed sideways. In a flash my problem was solved, and instead of digging vertically downwards, I dug horizontally sideways. It was indeed a maieutic moment, for I had discovered 'Horizontal Gravity'!

The phrase 'noticing the unnoticed' precisely reflects Newton's keen observation of how a falling apple demonstrated the first idea of 'gravity', and which now has to be termed 'Vertical Gravity'. This is to differentiate it from the 'Horizontal Gravity' as demonstrated by the rabbits. Note that both gravities had been there all the time and accepted as normal by apples and rabbits, but not so by the less perceptive humans.

Theories exist as to the relative influences of the vertical and the horizontal. Mr Harry Lauder in expressing that "It's nice to get up in the morning, but it's nicer to lie in bed" left no one in doubt as to his preference for being horizontal. This contradicts the view that the human upright stance is reflected vertically, and which, when reinforced by subliminal phallic considerations, induces a compulsion in us to build towers. A novel idea to illustrate this phallic philosophy would be to imagine the construction of a giant 'condom tower' made of rubber. If such an erection could be conceived it would help us to visualise our passion for vertical architecture. In the meanwhile the idea can be deflated and stored in french chalk.

It was at Callanish that I noticed that early humans had a tendency to quarry horizontal stones out of a cliff, so as they could stand them up later. They dragged them for a mile or so across rugged country before regimenting them vertically to become ancient monuments for some mystery as yet undetermined. If I had been a stone I would have objected to this and would rather have been used for some more obvious purpose, like being part of a Hebridean black house, and getting back to some horizontal sleep in the strata of its dark smoky wall – but all that stand-up solstice stuff, no thanks.

Vertical aspirations are demonstrated by big towers such as the 'Eiffel', 'Post Office', 'Toronto', 'World Trade Center' – and so on, not forgetting 'spires', 'minarets', 'totem poles' and the likes. Horizontals seem to represent a more plodding sort of endeavour like looking for 'light at the end of tunnels', or 'crossing bridges when we come to them'. But if this route is not as starry as the vertical, there seems greater

prospects of arriving horizontally at a worthwhile earthbound destination, as opposed to the confident ascent of some doubtful verticality. The American artist H C Westermann once made a 'Suicide Tower' – a reminder to high-flyers that upward vertical confidence can lead to a downward vertical fall.

I have an ongoing love affair with the big Finnieston Crane in Glasgow. It is called a hammer-head crane because it is like a structural steel hammer shaft rising from the ground, with its head becoming flat like the letter 'T', and so the vertical changes to horizontal. It is built like the Eiffel Tower and likewise the Forth Railway Bridge, which is really a tower lying on its side. Its arches cry out to contain airborne restaurants and observation platforms like its Parisian pal, anything to ensure that it is always there and loved.

These architectural 'found objects' do not over-emphasise phallic aspects. Neither does a tower which rises vertically, then changes its mind, bends, and happily returns to earth again.

This self-cancellin tower confuses gravity

and is called an 'Arch'.

Towers were once built for dropping hot lead from their highest point with the drips landing in a bucketful of water to cool, the droplets to become lead-shot for shotgun cartridges. Shotguns are used for shooting down high-flying birds which, when full of lead, fall to the ground and thus demonstrate the effect of Newton's 'Vertical Gravity'. When the experiment is repeated by pointing the same guns at rabbits, the perceptive bunnies elude the sporting fusilade by running *straight* into, not *down* into, their burrows. Their prolific survival is due to 'Horizontal Gravity' and if proof is required, try to count the rabbits on the Mound of Invernochty...

Sideways is best!

# Breaking the habit

*"... At the beginning of a pestilence and when it ends, there's always a propensity for rhetoric. In the first case, habits have not yet been lost; in the second, they're returning. It is in the thick of a calamity that one gets hardened to the truth in other words to silence."*

I WAS reading these very words from *The Plague* by Albert Camus when, by some immense and mystic coincidence, my wife interrupted to tell me the shocking news about the innocents who died in Dunblane. The terrible truth insisted on silence, and that silence still prevails.

Never in my long lifetime have I known all of the mishmash of rhetoric to cease with such suddenness. Within me a silent bell still tolls, insisting that the meditative calm remains, and placing a responsibility upon me.

I somehow believe, perhaps wrongly, that

being exercised by the arts we should have heightened perceptions of the frailties of the human condition, and so at this calamitous moment I have to take honest stock of my own aspirations. Let no-one say that this is the clichéd 'knee-jerk' reaction, but instead, an immediate and accurate focusing of inward thoughts already existing, so far only mildly expressed and thus comparatively ineffective in a world which seems intent on celebrating, even hyping, its own absurdity. Sure, sure, sure – there has been lots of chuntering within and around the art world, but that is all that it has been. Like mad cows we unquestionably allow ourselves to be fed on our own art, and the deadly disease is visual rhetoric.

Like any good public relations outfit knows, this art can be neatly packaged, sold through the customary ga-ga outlets, and help dilettante careers to make a strange sort of profit. I've a strong feeling that the aforementioned clear-minded Albert Camus would have agreed that such glossy activities have nothing to do with art, but instead, the very notions that real art should subvert. The counterfeit comedy is in fact a stage-managed tragedy – at least to anyone who thinks that art has the potential to begin to enlighten a deranged world – something it can never do when contaminated with perverse spirit.

This brings me to the British Art Show of which I will say only this. As an *aide mémoire* Douglas Gordon's *Trigger Finger* – a simple video satire illustrating how repetitive strain injury can be self inflicted by pulling a trigger too often, reminded me of Voltaire's Candide remarking "I've got into the way of killing people". Still thinking of Dunblane, it helped prompt my conscience to write what I'm writing.

There are more ways of killing people than by running through Holy Inquisitors with the sword or with an agitated trigger finger. Look or listen to this media for all the latest on the big international massacre circuit and, nearer home, the *Big Issue* keeps us informed about slower killings – for death does not have to happen at a stroke, and the slower less dramatic method of induced poverty is sufficient... I pause here to observe one of our great nuclear subs heading out to sea... Yes, isn't that what Voltaire and

Douglas are saying? I thank them both – and the sub, for quietly reminding me that there are still hard truths to be dealt with.

Inevitably, slowly, persistently, the rhetoric is already returning... I listen for the silent bell.

How do we break the habit?

*ArtWork 80 June/July 1996*

# All the fun of the art fair

THERE'S got to be something special happening in Glasgow if someone tells you about it in Edinburgh, and that's where I heard about the Art Fair with big, bright and fancy tents creating a buzz in the city's George Square. Right away I've got to say that I'm not all that nutty about art fairs – even though I once profited from being in one in London. I keep telling myself that art shouldn't be a commodity and deserves more than the ga-ga approach, but a friend wanted to go, so I tagged along.

I'd never been to an art fair before, and got over my reluctance by telling myself again that it was my duty to broaden my artistic spectrum. Thus conditioned I entered the first tent of iniquity with a nod to the ominous garnish of large inflated haemorrhoids which bounced cheerfully over the entrance.

There's something about a tented enclosure

that pleasantly obscures the unpleasantries of life outside. Add to this soothing quality some jolly art and jolly folk and you are in a civic fairyland. Magic potions, common to all private views, were offered to banish tension and sales resistance and induce a careless mood for meandering amongst the fairy shops and chatting up the attendant elves and gnomes. The ambience seemed to call for hot dogs and candy-floss, but that is not the food of fairies and not quite the thing when looking at art. There was even an avant garde gallery with its own fairie shoppe saying something or other about something or other, and proving that art fairs do not dodge deeper issues. Here and there some of the toad-stools were flecked with red dots, indicating that all was going well in Glasgow's fairy-land.

It occurred to me that an opportunity had been lost by not using the column of the Scott Monument as the central pole to create a big top circus tent. This way the permanent public stat-ues left outside could have been part of the Art Fair along with the impermanent art inside – like the marriage of Heaven and Hell.

All the Fun of the ᵃʳᵗ ‸ Fair

London could easily do the same with Nelson's Column, and with the lions and pigeons inside together it would be better than a real circus. The big ferris wheel they once considered for the Millennium could be in there too – but lying on its side. It could be sponsored by the city as a monster roulette wheel and they could show us how to twirl it. It would be a social comment.

The bad thing about art fairs is that you can actually get to like them. The fairy fripper-frattery is so seductive that it happily corrupts, and in such a way that you don't know it's happening. Dammit, I had a great time at that Art Fair and it seemed that everyone else did as well. With all this art making us such a happy breed, it is becoming increasingly difficult to be miserable. This cheerfulness plays havoc with the dispensation of angst, and infringes the right of serious artists not to be happy about things.

The good thing about an art fair is that it's only there for a few days and the magic spell of enthusiasm has hardly had time to wear off before it has moved on to inflict itself on some other fairyland. It's all a bit like fast-food – well presented, seemingly enjoyable, but afterwards you still feel hungry.

Across the road from George Square is Julian's Gallery of Modern Art – but without the bouncing haemorrhoids. There's no sign yet of this show moving on. Puck is in charge, the resident Fairy Queen is Beryl Cook, and dammit, I still feel hungry.

# It's a bonanza!

"**G**LASGOW has smashed its previous personal best in attracting tourists thanks to a multi-million pound marketing campaign built around the city's Festival of Visual Arts".

Wow! This quote from a Scottish newspaper refers to a tourist jamboree which boosted coach tours, the B&B industry, and the printing of two-colour folded glossy brochures. Dammit, and here was me thinking that art was meant to go a bit further and have a shot at changing the world.

I concede that the bus drivers, landladies and printers have good reason to be grateful for the industry of artists – now categorised as the 'art industry'. I even created an arty rail disaster to help keep the trains running on the Fort William line, but come to think of it, this could help the big tourist spenders to by-pass Glasgow – although they'll be happy about it up north.

I like my native city but it is becoming

increasingly difficult to artistically pat Glasgow on the back. Maybe the art supply exceeds demand or the product isn't right, but if the art world is trying to change the unreal real world, you'd think everyone would be grateful for anything as long as it changes something. A 15-minute stop in a gallery shop stuffed with T-shirts, fridge magnets and dainty notelets is not what I had in mind. Art as bait for tourist traps will not change the world before the bus leaves.

One of the changes I've noticed is that we don't build much any more, and even when we do, we don't do it very well. That could be the reason why we seem so keen on design – but if we'd just stayed at being good at it like we used to, then we wouldn't need design festivals to show us how to make electric kettles instead of big ships. A festival poster says this about a chair "I hope that it is as confidently modern as it is comfortable to sit in". This worries me, for I'm inclined to slip off the ergonomic bent wire that seems essential in good design.

There is talk about an arts renaissance which some say is likely to happen when Scotland has its own Parliament. That will be fine if it

It's a chair as
nature intended

stays as a renaissance and doesn't get worse. Politicians and tourist boards are already figuring out how our culture should be, and it could even break out in Gaelic, in which case the Fort William line will be handy for getting to it.

But back to this business of changing the world – the big question for the artist is how do we do it in a more meaningful way than propping up bus tours, B&B and glossy brochures?

Tourist boards and travel agents know a lot about the world and they seem quite chummy – provided you're not trying to get a refund after a duff holiday. They had an international conference here and the same Scottish newspaper said their "jamboree will introduce Glasgow to the most influential group of travel agents in the world".

This most influential group will arrive in shiny Boeing 727's, stay in lush hotels, and will be armed with full-colour 32-page high-gloss brochures. They will be suggesting that we book a trip and have a shot at changing the world – but somewhere else. This is better than a 3-star renaissance, more than a 4-star jamboree… it's a 5-star bonanza

… I wish us all 'Bon Voyage'.

# Clan, place, work

A HEAP of suitcases was causing a commotion at Glasgow airport. They were all labelled 'Macmillan', and they swirled around the carousel to be eagerly reclaimed by kilted arrivals. The friendly frenzy was due to this motto – 'Miseris Succerrere Disco' – a clear indication that the Clan Macmillan was in town and about to descend on Finlaystone House, their ancestral home in pleasant Langbank some 15 miles from the city. For five days the advertised woodland walks and tea in the gardens would be secondary, for the family seat of the Macmillans was hosting a clan gathering – and how!

Their Latin motto has nothing to do with 'disco' as in 'discotheque' – but a smart Canadian Macmillan from McGill University suggested it meant the Clan of Miserable Dancers. That interpretation belied their exotic Highland dress and cheery banter, so I checked with Clan Chief

George Gordon Macmillan of Macmillan and Knap, and he said it meant "I learn to help the distressed".

It was easy for him to follow the family creed for he is a decent hard-working man, and his wife Jane is a very pleasant hardworking lady. Chief George is more at home with a chainsaw than a claymore, the proof being the absence of one finger, and provided he isn't carrying a chainsaw I'd be happy to follow him into battle anywhere. With no battles imminent, the clan could only fight amongst themselves for the privilege of washing the dishes, for this is a do-it-yourself clan and everyone takes their turn.

Fireworks were the visual fanfare for the start of five days of great Macmillan goings-on, upstaged in the morning by the friendly warmth of handshakes with the kilted chieftain himself. The clan was then eager to know about heraldry – a dry subject easily put right by a visit to a handy distillery in the afternoon. Moistened thrapples lubricated their conviviality and in this congenial ambience tartan bow ties and high heels with buckles were perfectly acceptable, and so by not worrying about it, dignity survived.

There was no escape from the seduction of
tartan, even when the events switched from the
Highlands to the Lowlands for a Burns banquet
in the evening. I queried this, and the smart
Canadian reminded me that there is a sept of the
clan in Galloway – it seems they know everything
in McGill. Non-Macmillans weren't invited to the
big night out, so the wonder of that scene could
only be left to the imagination of mere outsid-
ers... But I know this... there was a splendid
marquee, three crystal chandeliers, and the wink-
ing lights cross the Clyde transformed Langbank
into a Mediterranean resort. On the groaning
table there was a regiment of 1996 Macmillan
blanc and Macmillan rouge awaiting the arrival of
a Macmillan-sized haggis which was sweating
amber beads at the thought of the clan chief's
chainsaw.

It is a tribute to the stamina of the clan that
next day they managed to board buses and travel
to Perth to re-enact the historically elusive 'Battle
of the Barrier' of 1396. This was fought between
the Macmillans and the McIntoshes who won.

How do I join?

This little-known historical fact was provided by the smarty from McGill. The mock battle took the form of a bicycle race, for wasn't the bicycle invented by Mr Kirkpatrick Macmillan of Dumfries in 1839? A reproduction of this bike finished a terrific second. If a McIntosh bike came in first nobody mentioned it.

It is possible that the Macmillans lost the 'Battle of the Barrier' because everyone had heard them coming. The clan's ceremonial parade through Perth was also unmissable. First a policeman, next a pipe band, then the reproduction bike, followed by the chief with his claymore held high with his wife Jane by his side, then the rest of the clan – all with holly in their hats. A spare pipe band marched behind, and lastly a policeman keeping his eye open for unsheathed chainsaws.

There was, however, blood on the hands of the chief, because even without a chainsaw he had managed to have his finger bloodied when he was walloping in the tent pegs with a mallet. Bandaged but unbowed, he responded well to medicinal claret.

In the evening it was back to the marquee and the Macmillan ceilidh with clarsach, fiddle, accordion, and on-the-beat hand claps. A keyboard tinkled ceilidh cocktail music for the transatlantic Macmillans. There were white heather hands on hips dancers from Glasgow, the Macmillan overseas choir comprising voices from New Zealand, Holland, Canada, Texas and Tennessee. Their bus driver from nearby Paisley quite naturally joined in and later obliged with *The Flower of Scotland*. All was well and afterwards they all fought again to help Jane with the washing up. The chief's bloodied finger was not a problem for the claret had done a great job.

... And what has all this got to do with art? Well, wasn't this a great family celebration about pilgrimage, performance, nature, music, and the relationships between '*folk*, place, work', as espoused by our own Patrick Geddes who re-adapted *Le Play*, the French sociologist's '*family*, place, work' – and all with the same unavoidable synergy so warmly reflected by Robert Burns. It is real, not just talk, it exalts the human spirit. Be sure his silent presence in Langbank would extend it to... *'clan,* place, work'

On the Sabbath, under the aged John Knox Tree in the Finlaystone garden, they all gave thanks to the great clan chief in the sky. Knox had preached under its branches in 1556. John B Macmillan, the Canadian from McGill whispered "The tree might not be that old".

...Says I, "Never mind the age of the tree JB, how do I join the clan?"

# No beginnings in the offing

JUST what is meant by a 'New Beginning'? This phrase gets bandied around a lot and has become a cliché for so many aspirational adventures. This could be happening for several reasons and perhaps it's because we're not happy with the way things are at the moment. Another reason might be that it has something to do with re-arranging what has been fine up until now, but unless dismantled and re-organised someone would be out of a job. The trick here is to create the illusion of progress and hide the cost of the transition back to where it started.

In the art world there are often events described as 'New Beginnings', when all that's happening is that someone has dreamed up a slightly different concept for their next brochure. If they called their project a 'New Concept' that would be fine, but they should understand that a mere concept falls far short of that state of profundity required for a 'New Beginning'.

I'm all for changing the world, and the late great Joseph Beuys had a meritorious shot at doing what he could. On one of his prints featuring himself and Edinburgh's doggy sculpture 'Greyfriars Bobby' there appeared these words – 'New Beginnings are in the Offing' and maybe that started it off. I was impressed at the time but later I began to think his optimism required clarification. Everyone knows of Beuys's other statement – 'Everyone an Artist' – another altruistic declaration also encumbered for universal acceptance by subliminal simplicity. It seems we need spelt-out slogans for exciting our intelligence, and if he had said – 'Everyone with the soul of an artist', it would have reflected his aspirations more than the misconstrued interpretation that we should all grab a paintbrush and start daubing.

Simplicity seems to have got in the way of Beuys's plea for the 'offing' of the 'New Beginnings' that he had in mind for extending concepts of art and as yet undefined. Yes, simplicity can be complicated.

The late Norman Buchan MP was probably the best Arts Minister we never had, and he once told me that progress was made by nudging. Beuys's work certainly nudged some of us, and I suppose that was towards a 'New Beginning'. Now I have to pass on the nudge to others – and so on and on. If we are really going to change the world it will problably be by a continuity of nudges, which leads us to Brancusi's 'Endless Column'.

You will know that his column's aspiring verticality is a sort of zig-zag of short equal legs which, like a free-standing graph, can easily be interpreted as a series of ever upward nudges. My complaint about his column is that all the nudges are shown as being equal, and unfortunately this cannot be. For example, the art of Beuys is a more positive nudge than say, Beryl Cook's. There are also negative nudges as well as positive nudges to contend with, and these would show up as U-turns in the ascending column. The positive aspect of these deviations is that it makes the artist reconsider the strategy for

63

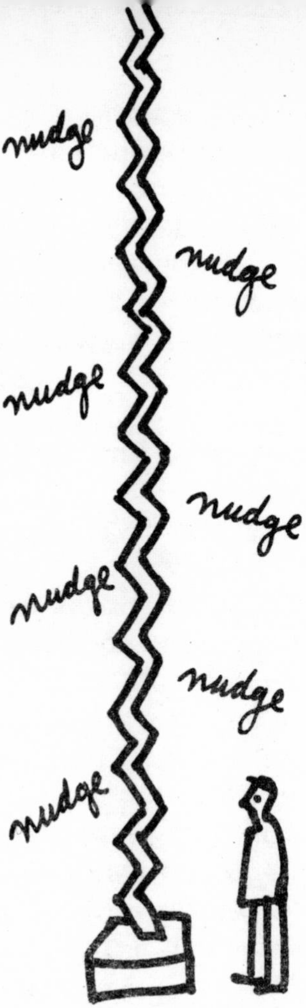
nudge
nudge
nudge
nudge
nudge
nudge
nudge

subversion, and this can generate re–invented strength for another upward nudge. This is art as I know it.

Carl André is a shrewd artist and his nudges come in kit form. I wish I had the guts to pounce on his pile of static bricks and re-arrange them as a column. However, by simply studying the tidy pile it is still possible to mentally assemble them as a concept. This way you will not get a row for touching them, which is one-up for conceptual art and peace and quiet for the Tate attendants. Your concept can have them ascending with as many positive or negative nudges as you care to imagine in the endless battle of equal and unequal zigs and zags.

If we could only find a magical bricklayer the bricks could be cemented upwards so as to wiggle their aspirational way to something better than that lying below. If such a column could ever be straightened out, it might, but only might, be heralded as a 'New Beginning'.

The great band-leader Count Basie, who only nudged with his eyes and a wiggle of the forefinger, used to call to his orchestra at the end of a tune – 'One more time!', and after playing a bit more, he sometimes re-repeated himself – saying 'One more time... one more time!'. This was to let his musicians extend what had already been appreciated.

As far as I know he never said... 'New Beginnings'.

# Here's to uncertainty!

IF THERE'S one thing you can be certain about it's uncertainty. Once upon an earlier time I never even thought about uncertainty, and this may simply have been due to the blind exuberance of youth, or just because everything seemed to be certain. When we were a manufacturing nation, we were all much busier, and probably that's why things seemed less uncertain, or more certain – take your choice. The 'Situations Vacant' columns listed plenty of jobs, and if you were a job seeker, it was most likely that you'd find some sort of work. In short, certainty scored higher marks than uncertainty.

Nowadays it appears that the inverse applies. There is more energy going a-begging and lots of it just gives up, for it doesn't like being discarded. The conditions are now right for brewing uncertainty, and when curt commands on headed notepaper arrive to suggest you re-apply for your old job, it induces added tensions in a depleted work-force commanded by a frustrated management – often mindful that they could be next. Thrashing about for a solution is like looking for a slither of soap in a bathtub. We chase the bubbles and complain, and uncertainty gets a bad name – but could it be undeserved ?

"Necessity is the mother of invention" is an optimistic phrase to whistle up the bright side of uncertainty. It suggests that a necessity happening as the result of an uncertainty, can happily affirm that it has the capacity to induce the birth pangs of invention. Wonderful stuff, and note how the negative generates the positive!

Here's another one from Jean Arp, a French surrealist artist who rejoiced in uncertainty. He said "I like miscalculations for they offer more promising results", and this is a terrific tip for getting out of trouble when a painting or sculpture goes wrong. With this attitude anything from an unwanted dribble to a busted bust has the unpredictable potential to actually improve the work! This could be why Marcel Duchamp wasn't worried when the glass cracked

I'm forever blowing
uncertainties

in his 'Bride Stripped Bare by her Bachelors, Even', and why everyone's quite happy with the Venus de Milo having two broken arms.

It seems that great artists can capitalise on uncertainty and know that it can be a great motivator and an unsurpassed incentive for making progress. Consider the uncertain Robert the Bruce having his mind made up by watching an uncertain spider in an uncertain number of caves.

You will probably say that all of this is OK in art and myth, but what about the real world? Most art is happy to bounce this way and that way on a trampoline and over a safety net, but this also develops the muscles for dealing with absurdity, and can generate a persistent resilience which the real world finds difficult to acquire. By way of an example, I'll now dismount from my bouncing hobby-horse and challenge a big-time absurdity to deride its negativity and bronco-bust it into being aspiring and positive.

...Consider that solar, planetary and human energy exists in profusion to nurture the totality of our being.

...Consider the absence of equity in the man-made absurdity devised for sharing common wealth.

...Now consider the unquestioned certainty and authority we allow to those who control it.

And next, the unquestioning uncertainty in the minds of those who are controlled, that is... ourselves.

These considerations will only frighten those who cannot un-believe that which is mistakenly believed to be certain.

In time, when the rejected emerge from their cardboard dwellings and *insist* on the negative becoming positive, then surely the alternative to the past miscalculations must at least yield another uncertainty of more promising results.

...Here's soap in your eye!

# A ferry story...

O N THE tip of the Mull of Kintyre there is an incised footprint on a stone. It is the footprint of Columba – allegedly. The Saint undoubtedly passed that way on his travels from Hibernia to Dalriada and perhaps he paused for a while on that stone to cool his feet. This would have allowed a sculptor monk a great opportunity to scribe a line around one of them, and then to chisel out the Saint's footprint for posterity.

It is a nice thought, but it is unlikely that nowadays a dignitary of any church would pose on a suitable rock and have a sculptor on stand-by to mark out one of his feet. A modern equivalent would be the Chinese Theatre in Hollywood, where a similar technique and adulation was accorded to movie idols who made footsy impressions in wet cement. It could, of course, be none of these possibilities, but merely an organic curiosity chiselled by time and weather – or even by some laddie in bygone Campbeltown having a daft wee joke with us all.

Whatever the reason I'm all for it, because it is not a boring thing to do on Kintyre – and anyone who says that it is, has no idea of the value of such ancient marks to the tourist board. A mark like this will arrest the interest of a wind-swept group of tourists for fully ten minutes before their attention span is drained. The regularity of time-squandering debates over the uncertainty of the footprint is a clear indication that a sense of mystery still dwells within us, and it is good that the footprint never gives the game away – something it has learned from Callanish.

Saint Columba established the first roll-on/roll-off service from Antrim to Kintyre. There is now a new modern ferry sailing from Antrim to Kintyre, and this is an up-date on the early route initiated by the intrepid Saint who must also be given credit for the first Isle of Mull to Iona service. We are inclined to think that MacBrayne or Calmac were the pioneers, or even Saint Demarco – but not so, Columba was first – albeit that Demarco was martyred by the Scottish Arts

Council for making too many voyages. It seems that they didn't understand the difference between the visionary art of pilgrimage and the art of private views.

These days, a sculptor monk would find it difficult to select the right tourist for a pilgrim footprint. There are so many to choose from and it has got be chiselled quickly before the attention span expires and their bus departs. Now, with the Skye road bridge, it's 'Over the Tarmac to Skye' – and the situation could get worse for there is now talk of building a road bridge over to Iona.

…But even on that holy isle, I have to say that I cannot imagine any sculptor monk – or even a daft laddie, chiselling away at the tyre track of a tourist bus.

…Do *you* believe in ferries?

# The Millennium blister

IT SEEMS that right through history the aspirations of the human race have nearly always been sculpturally or architecturally expressed by vertical structures. Look out of your window and there's every chance you'll see a church steeple. Add to this totem poles, minarets and corporate towers, all sprouting from the earth's surface. If this continues our planet could end up as the cactus of the cosmos.

After a bad start with their daft ferris wheel, London is going to break the vertical habit for us by aspiring horizontally – or nearly horizontally. You may remember my earlier reference to 'vertical gravity' as proved by Newton's apple, and the discovery of 'horizontal gravity' by the rabbits of Invernochty. It seems that this new design relates to the rabbits, for I refer to the flat-chested curve of the 'Millennium Dome'.

This structure is not so much a dome, but more as though the paint on the surface of the planet at Greenwich is beginning to bubble, suggesting that this low-rise curvature is a 'millennium blister'. Admittedly the structure is supported vertically around its perimeter by guy-ropes from tall poles – like giant cocktail sticks of architectural trendiness, and if each one spiked a cherry it could be conceived as a whopper birthday cake. It'll look great in the winter when iced with snow – but I'd stand well clear of the guy-ropes.

Am I alone in thinking that the year 2000 is not beckoning many of us for the ultimate vertical adventure into outer space? With the exceptions of MIR, the space shuttle, and sci-fi promotional videos, I am not conscious of a rush to buy telescopes or practice space-walks at the local baths. The preference for the walkman over the spaceman prompts the big millennium question … where does space exist?

The rabbits of Invernochty have always understood sideways space, and this could be the sort of space that the millennium blister will demonstrate. Once upon a time in a DC Thomson publication there was a sideways adventurer called

-it's in the right direction

'The Black Sapper'. He was the patron saint of rabbits and he travelled through inner space, which means under the ground. He wore goggles and a black skin-tight dry wet-suit, and he burrowed into this inner space in his one-man earth-boring machine which was like a giant screw-nail. He once bored through the floor of a conference room – right through the mahogany table around which plotters were plotting and he scattered them. He did this sort of thing in the 'Rover', out every Thursday.

The surprise of the 'Millennium Dome' is its deliberate flatness and one has to ask, is its blister profile designed to aspire us to colonise where so far only rabbits have dared to tread, vertically downwards, into inner space?

Don't worry, the 'Black Sapper' is down there somewhere and he'll keep us right, but it raises the question …is Newton's apple being superseded by a lead balloon?

# The adulation of the mediocre

JUST as a drip of water can wear a stone, the effect of what I am about to write will be equally imperceptible – but I'll write it anyway. I have probably lost my cause before I state it – but I'll state it anyway. I do so with reticence, for my pessimism assures me that my complaint will not change a darn thing, but I'll be out with it... *I'm not all that keen on Elton.*

This statement of low appreciation might have got by until I heard and saw him embarrassing that lovely piano in the Abbey with the candle song. That did it for me – maybe because it was so near to poet's corner – but whatever, I now have to revise my earlier generous opinion. I cannot tell a lie... *I find it impossible to take to Elton.*

I know I'm up against the whole world in saying this, for wasn't the whole world there on a

Elton

televised evening with him – and didn't he twiddle that celebrated world around his stubby less-than-an-octave fingers – and didn't the camera angles, spicy interjections, and on-stage lemmings so unquestionably indicate global approval – eh? ... *I just can't understand why I am the exception to liking Elton.*

I was once a paid up member of the Musicians' Union and liked playing in big bands. Big band musicians had certain musical skills, like being able to read the band parts even when their alcohol intake might have suggested that this was not possible. The command of their instruments was such that they could dismantle their music stand and pack it away whilst playing the National Anthem with one hand. They also possessed a certain candid quality which was evident when describing their musical inferiors – such as having 'cloth ears', or in the case of piano players, of 'playing the notes in handfuls'... *which brings me back to Elton.*

His vocal contribution unfortunately, cannot be ignored. When someone like him took a vocal in front of a big band, the brass and the saxes got their chance to have a quick slurp from a concealment behind the band parts, or relate the punch line of a dirty joke commenced during the previous vocal... *this way the musicians could be in harmony with guys like Elton.*

OK, I know I'm being tough on Elton, and there are other acolytes whose sparkle exceeds their talents. Is the fault, dear Brutus, not in our stars but ourselves?

But I digress, all I really want to do is question the mystery of the massive hype, and ask why there is no erosion as the drip, drip of water touches the stone, but instead there shines this metamorphosis of glitter and spangles which dazzles the starry-eyed multitude to rejoice in the adulation of the mediocre... *but not me, Elton.*

A big band musician once told me that when the great jazz percussionist Buddy Rich was on his death-bed he was asked by his good wife if anything was troubling him. She leaned over to listen and Buddy is said to have whispered "Country and Western".

*...Maybe he hadn't heard about Elton.*

# Cruising down the river

I LIKENED Richard Demarco's 'Voyaging beyond the Bath-tub' to 'The Drunken Boat' – that is, Arthur Rimbaud's surreal poem 'Le Bateau Ivre' which recommends sailing downstream as you please. Its first line is… "As I was floating down unconcerned Rivers" and, until recently, I usually glossed over the irritation of the word *unconcerned,* but now it insists that I should understand its significance in this poem.

It is easy to think of the open sea as being cruel, but the unruffled motion of a river suggests a flowing tranquillity; but in his first line, Rimbaud puts paid to that notion. It appears he wants to emphasise that should you ever fall overboard when your boat is drifting down the stream, the plunge and the splash will be the signal shock to remind you that the river is truly unconcerned.

The poem should be read by anyone who

feels safe in their job, for it is a caution to the conceit of anyone who believes they are secure and indispensable. But Rimbaud is also a positive force, and his poem suggests some surreal exercises to flex the mind into an attitude which can help the distressed navigator to swim to the bank, and there to contemplate the inevitable continuity of uncertainties. He gives imaginative examples of the unreality of surrealism, but ends with a hard complaint about the real reality of those, say, who live in cardboard boxes.

If life aboard the ship has been particularly comfortable prior to becoming a victim of affluence, then the cold plunge will be all the more frightening – for the greater the height of luxury, the deeper the despair of the fall. Conversely, poor men hardly move from one state to the other, and, by virtue of there being nothing in it for them, do not feel moved towards remedial action. The victim of high-flying affluence, however, will have every reason to consider ways to overcome the fall. It is obviously preferable if this can be done prior to the tumble, but expediency doesn't work that way – anyway, the latter practice is usually overlooked by affluence in overdrive.

The accident of falling overboard, like the realisation that we are not immortal, does much to concentrate the mind. The priorities which arise at the onset of uncertainties might be regarded as expedient requirements for salvation. Do-ers of good works like, say, Andrew Carnegie knew how to handle the irritations of conscience by donations of concert halls and libraries. It was the same with the ancient Greek merchants who wanted to say 'sorry' to their gods by building small 'thank you' churches – but what about the populace? This brings us back to where we were, for as far as the punter is concerned expedient action is hardly worthwhile one way or the other.

Sound the French horns, for Rimbaud rides again! Clippety-clop, here he comes galloping to the rescue. I know you are wondering how he disembarked from his 'Drunken Boat', mounted a horse and rode so quickly through the 25 verses of his poem; but let me tell you that in surrealism anything is possible. Enough – back to the 'Drunken Boat' and the concluding verse

its poetic log-book...

"I can no more, bathed in your languors O waves, sail in the wake of the carriers of cotton, nor undergo the pride of the flags and pennants, nor pull past the horrible eyes of the hulks".

...Sound the horn! ...Look out for hulks! ...Remember the cardboard boxes! ...The River is, understandably, Unconcerned.